MILLION DOLLAR
STYLIST ®

MILLION DOLLAR STYLIST®

A Hair Stylist's Roadmap to Financial
Freedom in the Hair Industry

Marquetta Breslin

RMNC Publishing

Million Dollar Stylist / Marquetta Breslin – 1st Edition

ISBN 978-1-935020-25-7

Dedicated to my husband Ricky, my daughter Nya, and my son Cale.

"Don't look for society to give you permission to be yourself."

STEVE MARABOLI

Contents

CHAPTER 1: CHAINED TO THE CHAIR NO MORE! 1

YOU HAVE BEEN BRAINWASHED TO FAIL 3

YOUR FUTURE SUCCESS HAS NOTHING TO DO WITH HAIR 6

RESETTING WHAT YOU BELIEVE ABOUT YOUR OWN VALUE
TO THE WORLD 9

WHAT IS IT EXACTLY THAT YOU DO FOR A LIVING? 11

HOW MUCH IS MAKING SOMEONE FEEL GREAT REALLY
WORTH? 12

SPREADING YOUR VALUE THROUGH THE WORLD 14

THE MILLION DOLLAR STYLIST® 15

WHY YOU WANT TO BECOME A MILLION DOLLAR STYLIST® 17

HOW TO TAKE THE FIRST STEP TOWARDS YOUR NEW LIFE
AS A MILLION DOLLAR STYLIST® 18

CHAPTER 2: BECOMING A HIGHLY SKILLED STYLIST 22

THE GOAL IS MASTERY, NOTHING LESS 24

THE BRAINWASHING OF THE WORLD – MAKING THEM
BELIEVE THEY ARE SOMETHING THEY ARE NOT 25

WHAT IS MASTERY? 26

MASTERY IS <u>NOT</u> A DESTINATION. IT IS A WAY OF LIFE 27

MY JOURNEY TO MASTERY WAS <u>ANYTHING BUT</u> A
STRAIGHT LINE 29

WHY YOU DON'T SHOW UP TO BASIC TRAINING IN
HIGH HEELS 32

TURNING THE CORNER TOWARD THE HAIR INDUSTRY 34

THE CHOICE YOU HAVE TO MAKE TODAY 36

CHAPTER 3: TELLING YOUR STORY 39

THE REAL FORCE THAT POWERS THE WORLD 40

WHAT CAN HAPPEN WHEN YOUR "IDEA PACKAGE" IS
PERFECTLY WRAPPED 41

HOW COMMUNICATION CAN CHANGE A LIFE IN
AN INSTANT 43

THE SIMPLEST WAY TO BE AN EXPERT COMMUNICATOR 45

WHAT'S LISTENING GOT TO DO WITH IT? 46

IT'S NOT ABOUT WHAT YOU DO 48

FINDING THE MISSING LINK THAT BRINGS IT ALL
TOGETHER 50

THIS IS WHY PEOPLE WHO DID GREAT IN SCHOOL CAN
STILL STRUGGLE IN REAL LIFE! 51

YOU MIGHT CALL THIS A MESSAGE THAT'S WORTH
HEARING 52

WHAT SOME PEOPLE CALL THIS PROCESS 54

CHAPTER 4: TAKE YOUR MESSAGE TO THE WORLD 56

DING DONG, THE "GATEKEEPERS" ARE DEAD! 57

BUILDING THE "HAIR SALON" THAT NEVER CLOSES 59

WHAT EXACTLY IS THE PURPOSE OF YOUR WEBSITE? 61

BECOME VALUABLE TO PEOPLE BEFORE THEY EVER
BECOME CUSTOMERS OR CLIENTS 62

HOW TO SHIP YOUR EXPERIENCE AND SKILLS ALL
AROUND THE WORLD! 63

A VALUE-CREATING WORKOUT FOR YOUR CREATIVE
MUSCLE! 65

THIS IS WHAT THE WORLD CALLS V-A-L-U-E 66

MOST STYLISTS GET PAID FOR WORKING. MILLION DOLLAR
STYLISTS® GET PAID FOR DELIVERING VALUE 67

HOW TO BUILD A MILLION DOLLAR STYLIST® WEBSITE
SYSTEM 69

CHAPTER 5: THE MOST VALUABLE BOOK IN THE WORLD......73

THE ART AND SCIENCE OF POSITIONING 75

THE TOYOTA® AND LEXUS® STORY 77

THE GOOD NEWS AND BAD NEWS ABOUT POSITIONING 78

THE REASON YOU WANT TO BE GOOD AT THIS.............................. 80

WEREN'T WE TALKING ABOUT YOU WRITING A BOOK? 81

WHAT IT MEANS TO THE WORLD TO BE AN AUTHOR 82

WRITING A BOOK IS NOT HARD!.. 83

CHAPTER 6: IT IS YOUR TIME TO LEAD 85

YOU ARE HERE TO LEAD OTHERS: TODAY IS THE BEST DAY
TO START!.. 87

WHAT DOES LEADERSHIP HAVE TO DO WITH BECOMING A
MILLION DOLLAR STYLIST®?.. 88

HOW EXACTLY DOES A MILLION DOLLAR STYLIST® LEAD? 90

TRANSFORMING WHAT YOU KNOW AND DO INTO HIGH-
TOUCH, HIGH-VALUE OPPORTUNITIES FOR
TRANSFORMATION 92

EVERYTHING CHANGES WHEN YOU'RE ONE-ON-ONE OR
IN A SMALL GROUP.. 93

BUT HOW DO YOU DO SOMETHING LIKE THIS?.............................. 95

FINDING THE DIAMONDS AND HELPING THEM SHINE
EVEN BRIGHTER!... 96

HOW TO JUMPSTART YOUR OWN CREATIVE BRAINSTORM.......... 98

**CHAPTER 7: LIVING THE MILLION DOLLAR STYLIST®
LIFESTYLE** **100**

PURPOSE. PLATFORM. PRODUCT. 101

WHAT IS YOUR PURPOSE? 101

PURPOSE LIVES AT THE INTERSECTION OF YOUR PASSIONS,
YOUR TALENTS, AND THE NEEDS OF THE WORLD 103

WHAT'S A PLATFORM? 103

YOU GET PAID FOR SOLVING PROBLEMS 107

"HEY, I REALLY LIKE WHAT YOU'RE SAYING HERE. I KNOW YOU
KNOW WHAT YOU'RE DOING, SO HOW CAN YOU HELP ME?" 109

WHATEVER YOU DO, NEVER FORGET THIS 110

ENJOY THE JOURNEY, EACH AND EVERY STEP OF IT 111

ABOUT THE AUTHOR **112**

"Definiteness of purpose is the starting point of all achievement."

W. CLEMENT STONE

1

CHAINED TO THE CHAIR NO MORE!

All I ever wanted to do was style hair. I love hair. I love talking about it, I love cutting it, I love styling it, and everything in between. Ever since I was a young girl growing up in Bunn – a tiny little town just north of Raleigh, North Carolina -- I've known that I loved working with hair. Doing hair was my dream.

My passion for hair began as a child when my mom or my Aunt Ella would straighten and curl my hair. After my hair was done, I would sit in front of the mirror for hours admiring their work. I loved my hair so much that I got in trouble in kindergarten for using my mirror and comb in class! Even at a young age, as you can see, I loved a great hairstyle.

I'm not the only one who's had the dream of becoming a hair stylist. In fact, if you're reading this, then my guess is that we share in that dream. Unfortunately, there's something very, very wrong with how that dream plays out for most stylists.

Instead of working hard and creating a life of freedom, fun, and abundance, most stylists end up finding themselves in a very different situation. They might be working hard, but all of that hard work isn't contributing to a better life. Money is tight, the hours are long, and there's really no end in sight. Every day is the same: work, work, work.

I hate to be the bearer of bad news, but for the average stylist there's just no way out of this hamster wheel. Hard work won't get you out. In fact, working *harder* is just going to make it worse.

What most stylists can't see is that they are in a prison of their own making. They are chained to the chair they thought was going to be their ticket to freedom. Instead, it is the exact opposite.

What most stylists can't see is that they are in a prison of their own making. They are chained to the chair they *thought* was going to be their ticket to freedom. Instead, it is the exact opposite.

If you've been to cosmetology school, then you'll want to listen to what I have to say because what I'm about to reveal to you could easily change the direction of your life – for the better. The truth is…

YOU HAVE BEEN BRAINWASHED TO FAIL

Cosmetology school trained you to fail. I know because I was there, and what I saw was absolutely terrible. Oh, I learned how to style hair. I learned the techniques, the processes, and the procedures. In fact, they did a pretty good job of walking me through everything I needed to know to pass State Board.

That's the problem. State Board gets you a license, but State Board has nothing to do with how to actually **make it** as a stylist.

I'm guessing that no one taught you about that – not the truth, anyway. They didn't teach it because they didn't know it. That's the reason that stylists spend upwards of $15,000 - $20,000 for cosmetology school, only to get out in the real world and barely scrape by making minimum wage doing hair. Don't you think there's something very wrong with that picture? If you're in that situation, you **know** there is something wrong.

I wrote this book because I've found another way. I've found a way to make it in the hair industry doing what I love <u>without</u> being chained to a chair 8-12 hours a day at a big box chain salon. I'm not saying that's a bad decision if that's the choice you've made and you're happy. If you enjoy that, then by all means continue, but I want you to know there's much more this industry has to offer to you.

I have to tell you that the journey has **not** been easy. I've made a lot of mistakes. I've hit a lot of dead ends. I've gotten tripped up time and time again. I was pretty much on my own to figure out a way to avoid the life of the average stylist.

It took me a little while to get the answer, but I found it. It would sound nice to weave some glamorous story about how everything fell into place just perfectly but it didn't. It took time and a whole lot of work.

The real secret for how I found the answer isn't much of a secret, but it **is** the truth. I simply refused to give up on my dream. I found a better way because I refused to settle for anything less than the type of life I know I'm meant to live.

Now, we probably haven't had the opportunity to meet, but I'm guessing there's something inside you that's not ready to settle for the life of the average stylist – the life where you work 15 hours a day, never see your family, and **still** can barely make ends meet. That's not a life. That's misery!

Your life is your responsibility. I believe that 100%, and that's why I don't waste any of my life blaming other people for my circumstances.

I've made it my mission to show you a better way. In the following pages, I'm going to walk you through exactly what that is. First, however, it's important to fully understand the problem and why it exists. Until you know why so many stylists are set up to fail, there's no way you can choose a different path.

Now, I have to warn you. What I'm going to talk about might very well sound like a conspiracy theory. Of course, anything is possible, but there's really no way to know for sure if the system is set up to purposely sabotage your career.

Really, it doesn't matter. Your life is your responsibility. I believe that 100%, and that's why I don't waste any of my life blaming other people for my circumstances.

Here's the first detail you need to know, and I can guarantee that you've <u>never</u> heard this mentioned in cosmetology school.

YOUR FUTURE SUCCESS HAS NOTHING TO DO WITH HAIR

Can you imagine an instructor in cosmetology school telling you that? Of course not!

Yes, you have to be good. Yes, you should aspire to be great. However, there are thousands of stylists who are good **and** great who can barely stay afloat, and it's not because they don't know how to style hair.

It's because how they've been taught to turn their skills into a great living is just flat out wrong! Cosmetology school shows you how to get licensed. Keep in mind, that's how they measure their success. To them, more licensed stylists means more success. Whether or not you succeed isn't something they care about, but it's your #1 concern, professionally, so here's what you need to know:

Your success in the hair business has everything to do with what's between your ears.

Anyone who's been through cosmetology school has to get rid of some of the B.S. that you picked up along the way. Otherwise, you're going to face some real mental obstacles.

Your success in the hair industry is controlled by your power and the depth of your belief about <u>what</u> <u>you</u> <u>deserve</u>. Let me phrase that another way. *You don't get what you deserve. You get*

Your success in the hair business has everything to do with what's between your ears.

---

what you believe you deserve. Each is completely different: one leaves your success up to luck, and the other puts you in control of your success.

I assume they never made this distinction while you were in training, right? Instead, I'm guessing you probably heard the same overly-used phrases I heard. You have to "put in the time" and "work our way up." Sound familiar?

I can tell you that **plenty** of stylists out there have put in the time – decades in this business – and still don't have much to show for it except more low-paying work and aching feet day in and day out. If you've ever watched the movie *The Secret*, which was really popular a while ago, you know it explained that you gravitate toward where you place your focus.

You don't get what you think about. You get what you believe.

Here's the distinction. You don't get what you think about. You get what you believe. In other words, if deep down you believe that working in a big box chain for the rest of your life is the best you can do, then that's probably the best you're going to get. It's very difficult, if not totally impossible, to create success in your life if you don't believe it can exist for you.

For example, if I told you that you could get paid $40,000+ for doing someone's hair a few times, you might think that's totally impossible. What if I said you could do that without becoming a "stylist to the stars" or becoming Oprah's personal hair stylist? In fact, you could do it with average men and women all over the country…. That makes it sound even more unlikely, right?

That's the problem. It sure does sound impossible. Let's be honest: if you went back to cosmetology school and told them that's what you wanted to do, they'd laugh you out of the building. That's because they don't believe it's possible, either!

And that's how it starts to go wrong; thousands of stylists complete cosmetology school brainwashed into believing certain fallacies about what they can and cannot do. However, I know a different way is possible. I know because I've **done** it.

RESETTING WHAT YOU BELIEVE ABOUT YOUR OWN VALUE TO THE WORLD

So here's a quick "gut check" for you. I want to make sure you're ready for the journey we're about to take together. If you truly think, in the very deepest part of your heart, that you are really only worth $10.00 an hour to the world, then the place I want to show you probably isn't something you're ready for.

On the other hand, if you know, deep down, that there **has** to be more to life – more for **you** in this life – then you are all set for what may be the journey of your lifetime.

Understand that my "gut check" has nothing to do with where you are right at this moment. You could be struggling like crazy to make ends meet, and that's okay because where you're at today has no control over what you do tomorrow. Don't let it get to you. It's not important.

What **is** important is what's inside of you right now. That's

When your client sits down in that chair, she's doing it for one reason and one reason only. She knows that what you're going to do will improve the future of her life in some way.

why finding that belief in you that you deserve better – that you're going to live better than the typical rat race – is so important. It provides the fuel and the direction for what we're about to do.

We're about to go somewhere that few stylists know about. I'm going to take you through each step of the journey. You certainly didn't get a roadmap to this place in cosmetology school. However, I can tell you that if you love doing hair and want to be successful in the industry, this is the place you want to go. In fact, this is where you want to live!

I'll tell you all about it in just a few moments. First, there's a question I want to ask you that's super important. You might think I'm crazy when I ask you this question. On the surface, the answer is going to seem brain-dead obvious, but stick with me here because this is important. Here's my question:

WHAT IS IT EXACTLY THAT
YOU DO FOR A LIVING?

Like I said, it sounds like there's an obvious answer, right? Well, I can tell you that the answer is far from obvious. I can also tell you that if you say something like "I do hair," then that's proof you've been brainwashed, and it's that brainwashing that we're going to clear out once and for all.

Think about this for a moment. Have you ever truly thought about the value of what it is that you do for your clients? The "system" would have you believe that "what you do" has to do with scissors and styling technique and product.

Yes, those are your tools that support what you do, but that's not really what you do. You may think that's what you're selling when your client walks through the door, but that's not what she's buying.

When your client sits down in that chair, she's doing it for one reason and one reason only. She knows that what you're going to do will improve the future of her life in some way. I'm sure you've noticed it with your clients. When they walk in, they have that "so-so" kind of vibe going. Sometimes they seem tired or run down or just not focused.

What happens when you've finished working with them? You see how they change, right? How they look in the mirror and instantly feel better about who they are? They walk out like a new person. They have a vibrant energy they didn't have when they walked in the door.

You might think you "just" do hair, but that's not what I see. What you do as a stylist is transform lives and change their perception of how they feel about themselves. It really is *that* big of a deal.

Your clients walk in feeling one way, and you send them out into the world feeling a whole lot better. When they feel better, they *talk* differently, they *act* differently, and they *expect* different outcomes. It's an extremely powerful gift to be able to give someone. Better yet, we get paid for it!

HOW MUCH IS MAKING SOMEONE FEEL GREAT REALLY WORTH?

Your clients are buying a *feeling*. If you remember nothing else from this entire book, remember that. Because that single secret will completely transform how you view yourself, and **that** will transform everything in your life.

When your clients come to you to have their hair done, what they are really buying is a new outlook on life. They are buying a better mood. They are buying your ability to transform them into a better version of themselves!

I will never forget my client Cindy who came to me emotionally broken from a cheating husband. Before she spoke, I could tell she had been through something, but I didn't want to pry into her business. I consulted with her, and we agreed on a full set of hair extensions. On the day of her appointment, I could tell she was nervous. I strategically placed her chair away from her mirror on purpose. Once I was finished, I turned her around and she burst into tears. She couldn't believe her eyes. She turned to me and said, "You just gave me permission to live again. You don't know what you've done for me!"

What I did for her is no different than what you're doing for your clients.

Just how much is that worth? I can tell you that it's worth far more than you're getting paid for it right now. This is why some clients out there at high-end salons might pay 10X (or more) than your clients pay you – even if the end result isn't all that different.

Your clients are buying a feeling. Scissors are just the tool you use to create that end result.

It's about the feeling they get with the stylist they like. It's about how that time spent sitting in your chair completely changes their outlook on life. That's the business we're in as stylists. We change people's perception about themselves, and we do it every day.

SPREADING YOUR VALUE THROUGH THE WORLD

If you want to be really successful, you need to understand that what you do is extremely valuable, far more valuable than what you're probably getting paid. The challenge is that stylists have never been taught how to truly see the value of what they do and how to communicate that to a client.

But, remember, there's also something else – another way to think that I guarantee no one ever mentioned in cosmetology school. What if there was a way to give thousands of women that "feel-good" emotion without ever touching their hair? If you could do that, there'd really be no limit to what your life could look like.

Remember, the more valuable you become to the world, the more the world will give you in return. It's a universal law, and that brings us to the point of this entire book – to introduce you to a world where your possibilities are endless.

It's a world where just about anything you want can happen. It's a world where you control your future in the hair business. No one else will control your destiny! Best of all, it's a world where you have the freedom and the resources to live your life exactly as you see fit.

Once you enter this world, you will never again be "chained to the chair" and forced to work for peanuts just to scrape by! I know this new, better world because that's where I live, and I'm excited to give you the directions you need to get there yourself. What I'm talking about is the world of...

THE MILLION DOLLAR STYLIST®

Now stick with me here because if you're sitting there right now struggling from month to month, you may think that believing you could be a millionaire just from doing hair might be a little bit of a stretch.

Becoming a Million Dollar Stylist® is about much more than money. Money is the last piece of the puzzle, not the first. Money is what happens *as a result* of getting the other pieces of the puzzle right.

Understand that when I talk about the Million Dollar Stylist®, I'm talking about a certain way of being in the world. I'm talking about a certain way of speaking and a certain way of thinking.

Being a Million DollarStylist® is about understanding the true value of what you do and then building a world around you where people value you in the same way. They use that value to improve the quality of their lives, and they pay you for it!

Being a Million Dollar Stylist® is about understanding the true value of what you do and then building a world around you where people value you in the same way.

There are two strategies you need to do and know in order to enter the world of the Million Dollar Stylist®. The first one is a commitment you have to make to yourself. Building the life of a Million Dollar Stylist® requires that you do what you have to do to live as the best version of yourself. This doesn't require money, luck, or anything else. All it requires is a decision to be better **tomorrow** than you are today, and all you need for that is a willingness to start.

You begin to act, speak, and think like a Million Dollar Stylist®. Then, over time, your life begins to reflect those changes.

The second strategy is that you need to have a roadmap. Here's the good news: you're being given one in the pages of this book. I have to tell you that I didn't have a roadmap for how to get to the world of The Million Dollar Stylist®. That's why it took me much longer than it should take you. I had to make a lot of mistakes that you will be able to avoid. I had to learn a few important lessons through trial and error.

WHY YOU WANT TO BECOME A MILLION DOLLAR STYLIST®

There's a long list of reasons why you want to become a Million Dollar Stylist®, and I'm going to give you a couple of them in a minute. But first, I want you to just take a moment and imagine your dream life. Make the picture in your mind as clear as you can. Fill in the details with color. Add the feelings. What do you feel like in this life?

If you've never done anything like this, really take some time to do this right. This is your life we're talking about! Really make sure you know all of the great things you'd like to be in it.

First of all, imagine clients **calling you** all day long to schedule their next appointment. The waiting list is so long to book you that there's no way you could possibly keep up, even if you were working 24/7.

However, you're a Million Dollar Stylist®, so you don't have to "chain" yourself to the chair anymore to provide for yourself. In fact, you only work with five clients a week! You get to pick the best ones, and you can pretty much charge whatever you like.

Even though you won't be standing behind the chair 24/7, the income will continue to come in and continue to grow. That's because you won't be living your life like every other stylist out there. You'll have access to a completely different mindset and blueprint for making it in the hair industry.

You can make your own hours…. You can choose who you work with…. You can choose your level of income…. You can do work once but get paid more than once…. You can put the quality of your future into your hands, not anyone else's…. You will be living the life of The Million Dollar Stylist®!

HOW TO TAKE THE FIRST STEP TOWARDS YOUR NEW LIFE AS A MILLION DOLLAR STYLIST®

At the core, being a Million Dollar Stylist® is about the person *you become* on the journey, not about what you have. Yes, having nice things is great. Being able to order food at restaurants without looking at prices is nice too.

*You must become valuable to
other people.*

However, this isn't about getting rich quickly because anything worth doing takes some time, and living the Million Dollar Stylist® lifestyle is worth doing. It's worth it even before the money shows up!

You become a Million Dollar Stylist® by giving the world a better version of yourself. In return, the world pays you back. I just have to warn you; once you embark on this journey, make sure you're prepared to experience some amazing transformations! Because once you begin offering more value to the world, you are going to be blown away by what can happen.

You can get everything you want in life if you first help enough other people get what they want. This is the true secret to success. You must become valuable to other people.

The good news is that you already *are* valuable. It's just that your value isn't packaged in a way where it can help a lot of people all at the same time.

Becoming a Million Dollar Stylist® will change all of that… and it will change your life. I've been on this very journey for years, and all I can say is *"Hold onto your hat! It's a wild and amazing ride…."*

If living the life of the Million Dollar Stylist® sounds good to you, then it's time to take the first step. In the coming pages, I've taken my journey over the past decade and organized it into an easy-to-follow "roadmap." The roadmap is designed to walk you through each of the steps of the journey to becoming a Million Dollar Stylist®.

The roadmap is going to show you the way to break free from the life of the average overworked and underpaid stylist and show you how to take what you love to do and use it to build the life of your dreams.

You might not believe that is possible at the moment. If you don't, that's fine. It's a lot to take in all at once, especially if all you've known is the "do your time and work your way up" method of success in the hair industry. That method just doesn't work, especially if you don't want to spend the next 20 years standing behind a chair working 15 hours a day.

The path to becoming a Million Dollar Stylist® is actually quite simple but it's not easy. If it were easy, then everyone would be doing it. If you look at the life of the average stylist, it's clear that they are not doing what I am about to show you.

The good news is that you are different. Something led you to pick up this book, and you're going to be very glad you did.

Because very soon you're going to have the complete picture in your mind of how your life as a successful stylist *could* be. Better than that, you'll know exactly what you have to do to make that dream a reality. ***So let's get started....***

2

BECOMING A HIGHLY SKILLED STYLIST

You were not put on this earth to play small. Playing small doesn't get you anywhere. Playing small doesn't add any of your unique value to the world. Worst of all, playing small cheats those people you are here to help. Without you stepping up to the plate to help them, they will live a life that is less than they deserve.

Most stylists think that what they do is cut, color, and style hair. On the surface that is exactly what they do, but that's only the beginning. It's barely scratching the surface. The truth goes much, much deeper.

If you've never thought about your career this way, what I've just said might not completely make sense. After all, I doubt that most stylists out there fully understand the responsibility they have to enrich the lives of their clients.

And that's a secret – to understand just how serious our role is. That doesn't mean we can't have fun. Goodness knows, I LOVE having fun. It's when you understand what a privilege and responsibility it is to play such an important role in someone's life, you act differently, you prepare differently, you think differently. That's the beginning of your journey to becoming a Million Dollar Stylist®. Living that type of life means that you are going to be thinking, speaking, and acting in ways that most stylists have never considered. This is really just the beginning.

A few minutes ago, I made a big deal that your success in the hair business has very little to do with how you do hair. I'm sure you know plenty of excellent stylists who are struggling to get by. Clearly, being awesome with hair isn't enough to build a successful business that can support the life you want to live.

But just because being great at styling hair isn't enough doesn't mean it's not necessary. Becoming a Million Dollar Stylist® is a process of transforming yourself into the person you are meant to be. That's why the foundation for your success as a Million Dollar Stylist® is the *quality of skill for doing hair* that you bring to the table. In other words, you have to be good at what you do, but, actually, it goes beyond your skillset – well beyond.

THE GOAL IS MASTERY, NOTHING LESS

Most people don't really think about the word "mastery" all that much. Isn't that something reserved for super-talented people in art or sports? Isn't mastery something that only a very few elite performers ever get to pursue?

The answer is NO. That's not what mastery is about, but before I talk about what mastery is, I want to make sure you understand what it isn't.

The opposite of mastery is **average**, and you don't have to look very far in today's world to find average. It's all over the place. In fact, it's *most* of what you see out there. People have been

Mastery is freely available to everyone. That's what makes it such a secret, really. Because even though it's "free," there is a price to pay to get it, and most people are simply not willing to pay that price.

brainwashed into believing average is okay. They've been told that average is the best they can do. Worse yet, they've been sold on the idea that they should be happy with average. After all, who are they to expect anything more?

This is why the world is in the state that it is in. Most people think the problem is the economy, their city, their employer, or events that are happening somewhere in the world. However, that's not the <u>real</u> issue.

Because all of those issues are simply the byproduct of something else, something that is far more powerful: the thoughts and feelings of billions of human beings. Thoughts and feelings are what create everything you see around you. Thoughts and feelings create everything in your life.

THE BRAINWASHING OF THE WORLD – MAKING THEM BELIEVE THEY ARE SOMETHING THEY ARE NOT

The problem is that we've all been taught that "average" is the best we can do. Obviously, this isn't true. I'm sure you can think of plenty of examples of people who have accomplished amazing things – things that are far from "average."

What's their secret? How do they achieve these things? Are they just naturally special people? Of course, they are special — just like you are special. Yes, perhaps they have an extra amount of talent in one area or the other.

There are plenty of people who have "talent" who never get anywhere. They spend their time talking about how talented they are and how they *should* be getting somewhere but they're not. That's because something very important is missing. It's something that no one else can give you. However, it's something that is freely available to every single person on this planet. That key is MASTERY.

WHAT IS MASTERY?

Isn't it funny that the very action that can open up enormous opportunities for you in your life is completely skipped over during the years we go to school?

It's sad, really, but I doubt you can recall any mention of the word "mastery" in all your years of schooling. I know I can't, so let me break this down for you because **getting this** could easily transform your future all by itself.

Mastery is freely available to everyone. That's what makes it such a secret, really. Because even though it's "free," there is a price to pay to get it, and most people are simply not willing to pay that price.

Mastery is the relentless pursuit of better. Always better. The concept that most people don't understand is that mastery is not a destination. It's not some place you ever arrive! Oh, people might look at your skills as a stylist and say, *"Boy, she is a Master with hair…"* or *"He has truly mastered that…."* However, that doesn't mean you stop. In fact, comments like that only add to your energy to pursue mastery even more.

MASTERY IS <u>NOT</u> A DESTINATION. IT IS A WAY OF LIFE

That's really the only thing you have to remember when it comes to becoming a highly-skilled stylist. If you're looking to "get somewhere" and "make it" so you can slow down and relax, you should realize right now that this journey never ends.

Mastery isn't a destination. It is a journey. It's a journey that you take on your own. Sure, you can get help along the way. We can all use that, but when you're walking the path of mastery, no one else really matters. This isn't about being better than everyone else. It's not about beating anyone.

No, mastery is about something far more important and far more powerful than simply how you stack up against other stylists. Mastery is about making a commitment to **you** being better tomorrow than you were today.

Living the life of a Million Dollar Stylist® requires a commitment to excellence. Again, it's not a contest, and it has nothing to do with anyone else. I keep saying that because we've all spent years and years getting trained to care about what other people think about us and to care about how we measure up to others.

My recommendation is that you do your best to completely delete that "program" from your mind. Mastery isn't about committing to others. It's about committing to yourself. I'm talking about you making the serious commitment to be the best version of yourself that you can possibly be.

The good news is that there has never been a better time in history to get access to all of the training and learning resources you could ever need to start your journey to mastery. I've spent the last 11 years of my life focused on creating resources that do exactly that. From DVDs to audios to books and to workshops, there are countless opportunities for you to become a highly-skilled stylist.

If you are highly skilled already, then keep going! Mastery isn't about rushing, and it's not about racing to the finish line. Remember, there is no finish line! It doesn't matter how long it takes. It only matters that you keep putting one foot in front of the other. You never stop because stopping would mean quitting. A Million Dollar Stylist® is not a quitter. The only promise you need to make to yourself at this point is that you will not stop, even when things get crazy. Believe me, they probably will get pretty crazy at some point.

MY JOURNEY TO MASTERY WAS ANYTHING BUT A STRAIGHT LINE

Remember, mastery is not just a word; it is a way of life. It's not always easy, at least my path wasn't. But before we go any further, I'd like to share with you a little bit about what that path looked like (so far). My intention in telling you a little bit of my story is to give you an idea of what this journey looks like and also to give you an idea of just how much potential you really do have to make an impact on the world.

You have this potential even if you can't see it at the moment. Looking back at my life years ago, I wasn't exactly the person voted most likely to succeed!

I grew up in a very tiny town called Bunn, just north of Raleigh in North Carolina.

Right away, I was interested in hair. My passion for hair began as a 6-year-old child when I taught myself how to braid hair on my Cabbage Patch doll. Everything I did from that age on, I somehow related it to hair.

From fifth grade through seventh grade, kids picked on me for my big eyes and my big teeth, and they made fun of me because I didn't wear the name-brand clothes that some of my friends did.

Needless to say, it was a tough time in my life. The teasing hurt at the time, but looking back I can see that my determination to rise above that experience helped make me a stronger person and the businesswoman I am today.

In high school I tried out for basketball, and I was so excited when I made it. After the first season, though, I lost interest and decided to try out for cheerleading. To my surprise, I made it and was the only freshman that made the varsity squad. I loved cheering.

Cheerleading became a passion of mine because it was so much fun! In fact, I ended up cheering and running track until I graduated from high school. However, despite my enjoyment for extracurricular activities, my high school years were bittersweet. My freshman year was a lot of fun, but my parents separated during my sophomore year and my grades declined. Then I lost my enthusiasm for school altogether. I still managed to pass my classes, despite the sadness I was feeling.

After graduation, my mom insisted that I get out of the house and go back to school, so I enrolled at Wake Tech Community College in Raleigh, North Carolina. I only attended two or three semesters before I dropped out due to transportation issues and lack of motivation.

Then I decided to visit my family in New Jersey. What was supposed to be a one-week trip turned into a one-year journey after I landed a job at the Novartis pharmaceutical company. That $12.65 was the most money I'd ever made, so I decided to stay and make as much as I could.

While I lived in New Jersey, I braided hair a lot, which at that time I didn't like to do because I wasn't that good at it. I just remembered back to when I started braiding on my Cabbage Patch doll – how persistent I was – and I saw that the more I braided, the better I got.

I applied that principle and soon had a small clientele. I was making a lot of money compared to the "nothing" I was making back home. Not only did I make a lot of money, but I also spent a lot too!

During this time in New Jersey, I also enrolled in Union County College, but I dropped out after my first semester. I found college to be just as boring as high school and completely pointless for me.

Once I dropped out of college, I got a second job at Circuit City, which I absolutely dreaded showing up to every day.

However, everything changed when I decided to join the United States Air Force in 1999.

Joining the Air Force was one of the best moves I've ever made. It started one Sunday while I was working at Circuit City and a gentleman came in dressed in an Army uniform. He shared with me some of his military experiences, and I knew almost immediately that I wanted to join the Army. Within a day or two, I called an Army recruiter and was on my way to sign the paperwork to enlist.

Then a few days before going to MEPS (Military Entrance Processing Station), my cousin's boyfriend came home from school and told me about an Air Force recruiter he had talked to. He gave me a lot of information about the Air Force and convinced me that I should change my plans and contact the Air Force recruiter ASAP – and I did.

The Air Force recruiter used my ASVAB (Armed Services Vocational Aptitude Battery) scores from the Army test to complete my enlistment, and on June 11, 2000 I left from Long Island, New York to join the United States Air Force. That day was a major turning point in my life because if I'd decided not to join the Air Force, I can't imagine where I'd be today.

WHY YOU DON'T SHOW UP TO BASIC TRAINING IN HIGH HEELS

I had no idea what to look forward to, but once I arrived at Lackland Air Force Base in San Antonio, Texas, I quickly learned what was expected of me.

Recruits – including myself – were bused to the base from the airport, and when the bus stopped the "fun" began. "GET OFF MY BUS!!!" were the first words I heard in basic training, which was intimidating, to say the least. I remember thinking, "What have I gotten myself into?" However, looking back, I remember having a lot of fun during basic training.

My family loves to hear the story of my arrival at basic training, so I'll share it with you too. I have always been a girly girl, and I was such a girly girl then that I didn't even own a pair of sneakers. In fact, when we were told to wear our civilian clothes to basic training, I naturally showed up in some high-heeled boots and a cute shirt! Today I wonder, "What in the world was I thinking?"

After exiting the bus, we had to form a line and march to a building that seemed like it was five miles away – and I marched in my high-heeled boots!

It's hard to connect the dots when you're looking forward in your life or your business. It's only after you've done it, when you look back, that everything makes sense.

My boots made so much noise that our Military Training Instructor yelled, "WHO THE HELL SHOWED UP FOR BASIC IN HIGH-HEELED SHOES?!"

I was so scared he'd come back there and torture me that I marched on my tippy toes the rest of the way. The upside is that it was the ULTIMATE calf workout!

TURNING THE CORNER TOWARD THE HAIR INDUSTRY

I soon became friends with a few of the recruits, and I started braiding hair for a couple of friends in our dorm. Before long, girls were asking me to cornrow their hair every night. The other girls in other dorms were wondering how we all looked so fly and managed to have our hair meticulously done. It was fun. That experience taught me that braiding hair for others was definitely something I wanted to continue doing.

After graduating from basic training, we went to tech school. The girls who came with me continued to ask me to do their hair, and I acquired quite a few clients between basic training and tech school. Some of my clients ended up stationed with me at Langley Air Force Base in Hampton, VA where I continued to do hair until I met my husband Ricky.

Ricky and I met in the dorms at Langley. We dated for eight months, and then we got married. Ricky saw that I was always doing somebody's hair in our tiny 600-square-foot apartment, and he decided to start a website to promote my hairstyling services. I was reluctant; I didn't want to jump into the business right then. However, ultimately I told myself, "Why wait? Let's just do it and see what happens." I've never once looked back.

In July of 2003, we started Braids By Breslin and put an advertisement on our car, and I started getting new customers right away. People loved my work, and I was really busy. Then, when Ricky came to me with the idea of teaching other people to braid hair just like I do, I was enthusiastic. Much to my surprise, Ricky had already done the research, and he was in contact with a film producer within hours.

Within three weeks, our first DVDs were filmed. To be honest, they were horrible. We filmed them several times, just trying to get them right. At that time we couldn't afford to get the DVDs mass produced, so we had the covers copied at Staples and burned the DVDs in our apartment.

THE CHOICE YOU HAVE
TO MAKE TODAY

As you now know, my road to pursuing mastery as a stylist was not exactly a straight one. Yours may not be straight, either, and that's fine.

If I think back through most of the events of my life, there's one thing I can say was true just about the entire time: no matter what I was doing, I always went out of my way to do my best. (Okay, there were a few years in school where that clearly wasn't true, but no one is perfect!)

I don't know if that's something I got from my mom or what, but I know that's inside of me. I also know that if you can find that within YOU, then there is nothing that can stop you.

It's hard to connect the dots when you're looking forward in your life or your business. It's only **after** you've done it, when you look back, that everything makes sense. That's good advice right there from Steve Jobs, the founder of Apple, the computer company. Yes, maybe you bounced around a lot from this thing or that thing, but it all worked together to get you where you are.

You know what? It doesn't matter where you are or where you've been. All that matters right now is where you're going from this point forward.

Before we go any further, here's the choice you have to make right now. **Are you ready and willing to make the commitment to Mastery? Are you prepared to do what it takes to become a highly-skilled stylist?**

I can't answer that question for you, of course. Only you can. However, committing to the Mastery journey is absolutely necessary in order to live the life of a Million Dollar Stylist®. Some people just aren't willing to make that commitment. I'm sure you've seen them around doing hair. Spotting them is pretty obvious, actually.

A highly-skilled stylist knows how to handle pretty much any situation when it comes to hair. If they don't know how to do something, a highly-skilled stylist will either figure it out or refer the client to someone who can help them. That is a commitment to Mastery… even when it means that you refer the client. In that case, your "skill" as a stylist is knowing where your skills start and stop and not being embarrassed to make decisions accordingly.

A stylist who is <u>not</u> committed to Mastery will take whatever comes his or her way, whenever it comes. That individual might not be prepared or qualified to handle it but will do it anyway!

It reminds me of this girl in cosmetology school who needed the tip money to support her drug habit. One day, she took a client who wanted to go from jet black to blonde in a single sitting. Now if you know anything about coloring hair, you know that this is simply not possible in one sitting with non-virgin hair. However, this stylist took the client and made the promise to do it anyway.

The stylist took her client's mid-back length hair and bleached it with heat. I'm talking flat iron to the foil type of heat. It was horrible! Guess what happened? Yep, the client lost **half her hair.**

Commit to becoming a highly-skilled stylist. It is not easy, but it is required if you're going to move on to the next level of living the Million Dollar Stylist® life. You can do it, and the world needs you to do it.

3

TELLING YOUR STORY

To say I am excited for you to read this chapter would be quite an understatement. The reason is simple: out of all of the valuable ideas in this book (and there are a lot of them), the ones you're going to discover in the next few minutes are the most powerful. Period.

Why is the material in this chapter so vitally important to your future as a Million Dollar Stylist®? It's because without the skill revealed in the next few pages, you simply will not have what it takes to make a major impact on the world. Please take your time as you go through the next few pages. Read every word. More importantly, think about what you are reading and how to apply this shift in perspective to your life and your business. What you're about to discover could very quickly change your life, just as it's done to thousands and thousands of others.

THE REAL FORCE THAT POWERS THE WORLD

Think about the people and the events in your life. Have you ever thought about what it is exactly that motivates those people to take action and what it is exactly that causes those events to occur? I've thought about it. I've thought about it a lot.

The answer is deceptively simple. The motivating factor behind just about everything that happens in this world is an IDEA. Ideas are what motivate people to take action. Ideas are the cause of just about everything.

You must understand how to communicate. You must understand how to effectively get an idea from one place to another. When you have truly mastered the art of doing this, there simply are no more limits to what is possible in your life.

Ideas are why people come into the salon to get their hair styled. In that case, the idea in their mind is that **after** their time at the salon, they will look better. Because they look better, they will feel better. Because they *feel* better, they will take completely different actions in their life than they otherwise would have taken. All of this from a single IDEA!

Here's the kicker: that idea in that client's mind didn't get there on its own. Every day, we are all bombarded with thousands of different ideas about thousands of different things. The crazy part is that *some* of those ideas have impact and others just disappear without a trace.

What makes the difference? The difference is the **package** in which those ideas were delivered. In other words, it comes down to *how* those ideas were communicated from one person to another.

WHAT CAN HAPPEN WHEN YOUR "IDEA PACKAGE" IS PERFECTLY WRAPPED

Now, I don't know if you're working right now as a stylist or if that's something you're working towards. At some point, as you get good, you're going to have something happen to you that you should probably be prepared for. Otherwise, it might be a bit of an uncomfortable situation.

The first time you have a client cry in your chair because of the work you've done can really catch you off guard. I'm talking about tears of joy here, not tears of sadness.

Why is that happening? Why would a client go to all of the trouble to schedule an appointment, come to the salon, and pay good money, only to end up in a jumble of tears?

As it turns out, an event like this is a perfect example of the type of impact that can be created when an **idea** that gets transferred from one person to another is "wrapped" in just the right package.

You may wonder, why, exactly, is my client crying? Here's why. She's crying because your work represents an idea that is delivered right into her heart. It's an idea that is so powerful that it creates tears… tears of joy.

What is this idea? It's the idea that your client is far more beautiful than she thinks. You've just helped give her the opportunity to be reminded of that and to help her share her beauty with the rest of the world. This is why being a stylist is such an enormous privilege and responsibility. What you are able to do, as a stylist, is create a profound impact in people's lives.

However, it all depends on your ability to develop one vital skill. You must understand how to communicate. You must understand how to effectively get an idea from one place to another. When you have truly mastered the art of doing this, there simply are no more limits to what is possible in your life.

Think back to someone like Oprah. What made her so successful? What allowed her to create such an impact on the world that it's being felt even now, years after she ended her daily TV show? The secret was her ability to communicate and do it in a way that, although she was talking to millions of people, made it feel like she was talking to YOU.

HOW COMMUNICATION CAN CHANGE A LIFE IN AN INSTANT

As I write this, I've just returned from a $15,000-per-person training event I want to tell you about. I bring it up because it involves a mentor of mine (yes, I am always learning, investing, and getting better) who is by all counts and measures a Master in the art of communication.

The amazing part is that this individual has not only mastered the art of communicating in words, he's also mastered the art of communicating <u>without</u> them. This means the impact he is able to create in the world is drastically multiplied. Not only that, the speed at which he is able to create that impact is nothing short of amazing. The reason I pursue true masters like this one is simple: I am on a mission to share my message with millions of people around the world. I want to free stylists everywhere from the mind prison we've all been trained to believe is the only option for us.

The simplest way to become an Expert Communicator is to develop the ability to truly understand what it's like to be in the shoes of the people you are trying to impact.

I want to show them that life exists outside of that prison – a life they can actually make a reality for themselves – *provided they invest the time and energy required to build it.*

The only limiting factor I can see at the moment is my ability to get that message delivered to the right people in the right way. That's why I'm focusing the majority of my effort on completely removing that limiting factor.

Let's get to the heart of how you become an Expert Communicator. It's really quite simple, but it's certainly not easy. If it were easy, everyone would be doing it, and it's clear that "everyone" is not cut out to be a Million Dollar Stylist®.

THE SIMPLEST WAY TO BE
AN EXPERT COMMUNICATOR

The simplest way to become an Expert Communicator is to develop the ability to truly understand what it's like to be in the shoes of the people you are trying to impact.

Most people's idea of communication is talking. They talk and talk and talk. Usually what they're talking about is the subject they find more interesting than any other thing in the world. That subject, of course, is themselves.

The big problem with this approach is that no one else in the world is interested in hearing you talk about you. Okay, maybe your mother or your father might sit there for a while, but even your family will have their limits.

As for the general public, they don't want to hear about you because all they're interested in is hearing about themselves!

Understand that talking is not communicating. You can talk until you're blue in the face, but that doesn't mean that anyone is going to listen or that your idea is going to get delivered to the people who can use it.

To be an Expert Communicator, the skill you need to master is one of the least popular, least sexy, least practiced skills in the world. That skill is the ability to **listen.**

WHAT'S LISTENING GOT TO DO WITH IT?

Stick with me here because if you truly **get** what I'm about to explain, then you're going to find your path towards the life of the Million Dollar Stylist® a whole lot smoother than most people.

Most people have no interest in figuring out what other people want. They're not interested in hearing about other people's problems, other people's fears, or other people's dreams. Again, we're all pretty much preoccupied with ourselves. It's just human nature to be wired that way. It's pretty normal.

However, if you're looking to live the life of a Million Dollar Stylist®, then **normal** isn't going to cut it. In fact, "normal" behaviors will most likely keep you from ever getting to where you want to go.

There is **gold** to be found in listening to the people you are trying to help. There is **gold** in truly hearing what your clients are dealing with and in understanding what they're feeling and where they're trying to go. There is **gold** to be found in understanding (maybe even better than they do) exactly what it is that makes your clients tick.

You know what happens when you can do this? When you make it clear to your clients that you "get them" on a very deep level, they look at you and think, *"Finally, I've found someone who understands where I'm at…. Thank goodness!"*

It's at that point that they open the door. That's the door that allows everything else you're saying to come right into their lives. They let you in, they trust you, and they like you. Earning that privilege from someone is an enormous gift and an enormous responsibility, but it doesn't end there. In fact, it's just the beginning.

Once you are sold on the **value** of learning to listen and you truly tune into what your clients and customers want, then you can really begin doing the work to get your message out to the world. There's a very special way to do it that will make the **impact** of your communication much, much greater.

Once you are sold on the value of learning to listen and you truly tune into what your clients and customers want, then you can really begin doing the work to get your message out to the world.

IT'S <u>NOT</u> ABOUT WHAT YOU DO

If you're going to be an Expert Communicator, you need to understand why some people get listened to and other people get ignored. We've already covered the fact that blabbing on and on about yourself is not the smartest move.

Let's take your average stylist. If you were a potential client and you asked him or her, *"Why should I come to your salon?"* how would that person answer? Well, my guess is the stylist would launch into a complete rundown of everything she can offer the potential client. Or, he'd talk about all of the services his business provides. She might even go into detail about how carefully she does this or how expertly she does that.

If this stylist loved talking about hair, the poor potential client might have a hard time getting the conversation to end! By the time it all stopped, think about what was accomplished. There was a **ton** of talking but very little communicating. Without the communication, nothing got accomplished.

Here's what you need to remember: no one is interested in what you do. People are only interested in what they <u>get</u> because of what you do. Read that sentence again because in that sentence is **the** secret you need to never forget when you're out there on the road to becoming a Million Dollar Stylist®.

If all you ever do is talk about what you do, you'll never become an Expert Communicator. However, if all you ever talk about is the **result** of what you do (which is all the client cares about), then you're going to have no trouble attracting attention.

Your clients want the result. They want to look better. They want to feel better. They want to go natural. They want a weave. They want extensions.

It doesn't matter **what** the result is (there are many) as much as it matters that you focus on it when you're communicating with potential clients. This single skill will make you stick out like a sore thumb among stylists, but you'll stick out in a **good** way because you'll be the only one speaking the language of the client!

Here's what you need to remember: no one is interested in what you do. People are only interested in what they get because of what you do.

FINDING THE MISSING LINK THAT BRINGS IT ALL TOGETHER

There's one more major piece we need to address if you're going to become an Expert Communicator. We've already spent a fair amount of time concentrating on the HOW of becoming an Expert Communicator. We've talked about the listening and how to package what you say in a way that's attractive to your potential clients.

Now, there's something else you'll need if you're going to make a major impact on people's lives. It's something we've been trained <u>not</u> to do much of in today's society. Therefore, as you get going, it might take you a few tries to get into the swing of this skill, but that's no problem. If you stick with it, over time you will become very good at it.

The education system we've all been through doesn't reward critical thinking.

What am I talking about, exactly? I'm talking about the ability to think for yourself. Think back to your years in school. Thinking for yourself didn't exactly send you right to the front of the class. In fact, "thinking for yourself" could very well get you a failing grade or worse… an afternoon in detention!

The education system we've all been through doesn't reward critical thinking. Critical thinking is when you look at something and are able to formulate your own opinion about it and be confident in it without getting validated by some authority figure. Just think back to high school. The only way you got good grades was to follow the teacher's orders and give the teacher the answers she wanted on the tests. Those answers weren't always the only answers, but they were the "right" answers because she said so, right?

THIS IS WHY PEOPLE WHO DID GREAT IN SCHOOL CAN STILL STRUGGLE IN REAL LIFE!

The real world doesn't work the same way that the school world worked. You can't act like you did as a student unless you want to spend the rest of your life taking orders from someone just like you did in high school. (Plenty of people do this, by the way, but Million Dollar Stylists® don't.)

Back to the idea of critical thinking…. Why is that so important for you as a Million Dollar Stylist®? It's because the ability to look at a situation and come to your own conclusions makes you more valuable and more interesting than the average person, but that's only the beginning of it, really.

If you're going to become an Expert Communicator, not only do you have to understand how effective communication works, you also have to have something interesting to say to the world!

Oprah had something to say to the world. She told the world that a black woman in this day and age, even with an extremely challenging childhood, can make it to the top.

Every day she got on TV and demonstrated that to millions and millions of people – and she went one step further. She used her platform to make it clear to her viewers that **they** could also do great things… no matter where they were in life at the present moment.

YOU MIGHT CALL THIS A MESSAGE THAT'S WORTH HEARING

That's what you want. If you're expecting people to listen, then you better show up with something to say!

I don't mean you need a speech. I mean you have to stand for something, and you have to live in a way that is congruent with what you stand for. My guess is that you already **do** stand for something. The fact that you stand for something is extremely attractive to a large number of people. You just might not know exactly what that is or quite understand the most effective way to make your message known, but you'll get there. You just have to get out there and start doing it and learning as you go.

To the average person, this can be scary – downright scary, actually. Because when you go out into the world with a message that needs to get heard, you're going to find some people who just flat out disagree with you. They might actually tell you that they disagree with you, or they might simply whisper it to their friends. For someone who was trained in the traditional school system, "not being liked" makes you feel pretty crappy. It's just not fun.

In the real world, you can't stand for something without having it turn off some people. In fact, if you go out there and find that everyone is agreeing with your message and how you're communicating it, it's likely that you're just not saying anything important.

Million Dollar Stylists® **know** what they stand for, and they are not looking for approval from anyone. They only have one goal: to communicate their message to as many people as possible as effectively as possible.

You are here to inspire and empower others. That's what we do. We take our experience, our perspective, our skill, our dreams, and vision, and we share them with people we can help.

WHAT SOME PEOPLE CALL THIS PROCESS

While I've been talking about communicating for the last few pages, there's another name for this process – a name for the process of packaging ideas and getting them to spread around the world and prompt people to take action.

That's what some people call M-A-R-K-E-T-I-N-G. If you're reading this book, you're most likely a hair stylist. That's what you **do**, but that's not the business you're in. The business you are in is marketing yourself as a stylist. That's completely different, and it's something we're going to talk about in more depth in just a moment.

Because the better your marketing skills become, the more easily you will be able to create impact.

How **many** people you can reach is really the question. Once you start to get clear on what your message is and what you stand for, the next step is to figure out how to **amplify** that message.

You want to be efficient, but the bigger priority is to be **effective**. You want your message to get delivered. If your message doesn't get delivered, it can't create change.

The good news is that there are tools now available to all of us to amplify our message and take it to thousands and thousands of people.

4

TAKE YOUR MESSAGE
TO THE WORLD

Twenty years ago, someone with the Million Dollar Stylist®
mindset didn't have a lot of opportunity to make an impact on
the lives of thousands of people.

Really, what could you do? You could maybe write a book and
get that in a bookstore. (Good luck!) Maybe you could get on TV
or the radio or something, but back then, even doing those things
required that someone else knew about you and was willing to
take a risk to publicize you and what you were about.

They might do that for a celebrity but what about just a normal
stylist? *Your chances would be extremely slim.*

The problem, really, was that there were tons of gatekeepers standing between you and the rest of the people in the world that you could help. Like most human beings, the gatekeepers spent a lot of time focusing on themselves. The number one priority of a gatekeeper is to do whatever is necessary to **remain** a gatekeeper. That means that taking risks and publishing books or featuring "unknown" people on TV weren't really chances they were willing to take.

The bottom line is that years ago, getting your message out to the world simply wasn't a very practical goal.

DING DONG, THE "GATEKEEPERS" ARE DEAD!

Okay, they're not literally dead, but I'm happy to say that they are pretty much irrelevant. In fact, almost every day you can see examples of the old style "gate keepers" becoming completely unnecessary. If you're a musical artist, you no longer need to wait to get "chosen" by a record label. You just start your own record label and start distributing your own music online.

The same thing holds true if you're an artist. You don't need to get picked up by a gallery. You just need to go out and directly find people who love your art. You don't need to ask permission, and you don't need to wait for someone to "let you in."

One of the traits of a Million Dollar Stylist® is that we don't wait for anything or anyone. I don't say that with an attitude; I just say it with an extreme level of confidence in what I'm here to do.

When you light that fire inside your gut that fuels your mission to go out and help people, "waiting" or asking permission to add value to the world just doesn't fit in the picture.

So, how do you do it? How do you take your story and your message and your services and share them with the world? You do it through the Internet with a very unique style of website.

The number one priority of a gatekeeper is to do whatever is necessary to remain a gatekeeper.

BUILDING THE "HAIR SALON" THAT NEVER CLOSES

I will never forget the day it happened. My husband Ricky and I were in the Air Force and were having lunch at Langley Air Force Base. There we were, sitting and chowing down, when the email came in. It was an order from our website. It was not just <u>any</u> order; it was our first order ever!

Our lives changed that day in that very moment. Although it might seem like I'm blowing it out of proportion, I'm not. That day, I realized I could make a living doing what I loved to do without having to stand behind a chair doing hair for 15 hours a day.

Now, granted, it was just <u>one</u> order. It wasn't even enough to pay our electric bill, but that didn't matter. It wasn't about the money. It was about what that order represented.

What it represented was a door to **freedom**. I walked through that door and I never looked back. Now I have the privilege of helping **you** walk through that door as well.

Imagine if you could build a new type of "hair salon" that was open 24/7. Every single minute of every single day, your "salon" could be helping people look great and feel great. You could be helping people on holidays, on weekends, even on your days off!

You might wonder how you'd staff a "salon" like this. After all, who wants to work on weekends or on holidays? Well, that's the best part about this "salon." Because even though it would be open for business all the time, you won't ever have to actually **be** there.

This is exactly how my websites work. I'm never there, but they keep on working anyway. They talk to people about my message, explaining what it is I do and how I do it. They offer products and services that can help my fellow stylists with a long list of issues in and around hair and beauty.

The best part is, my websites never get tired. They never have a bad day. They never call in sick. They're never even late to work!

That's the purpose of a Million Dollar Stylist® website. You create a system that builds trust with a large group of people. Then, with that trust in place, you offer those people solutions to the problems they have.

WHAT EXACTLY IS THE PURPOSE
OF YOUR WEBSITE?

Here's where the strategy behind being a Million Dollar Stylist® starts to go in a different direction from your average business person.

Most people might look at a website full of hair-related products and services and think that the purpose of that website is just to sell those things.

On one hand, that's true, but selling hair products is really a byproduct of something else that is far more important. It's something that's far more valuable than money. It is **trust.**

Without trust, you can't do a thing. **With the trust of a large group of people, <u>anything</u> is possible**.

That's the purpose of a Million Dollar Stylist® website. You create a system that builds trust with a large group of people. Then, with that trust in place, you offer those people solutions to the problems they have.

You're trying to earn the privilege of helping someone look great and feel great. So how do you use a website to build trust? The recipe is simple, but not easy. The goal is to use your website to…

BECOME VALUABLE TO PEOPLE BEFORE THEY EVER BECOME CUSTOMERS OR CLIENTS

This is what your website allows you to do. Just think about all of the knowledge you have when it comes to hair. Right now, all of that valuable knowledge is stuck. It's stuck inside your head where it can only help people if you decide to let it out.

Now, let's say you sit down one day and decide to film a video of you demonstrating a particular hairstyle. You upload that video to YouTube® and then you tell everyone who knows, likes, and trusts you about it. Word of that video spreads. Pretty soon, 50,000 people all over the world have watched that video and benefitted from your expertise.

Now think about how most stylists go about helping other people. They do it **one person at a time.** Can you imagine demonstrating the same hairstyle 50,000 times, once to each person?

That would be nuts, wouldn't it? Even if you could pack 500 people into your salon, you'd still be stuck demonstrating that hairstyle 100 times. Now, I love hair, but the thought of doing that would be enough to make me want to jump off a bridge! Think about it; a website can get the job done without you even breaking a sweat.

The best part is that you're not only going to make a single video. You can write articles, you can put together short booklets, or even record audio with you explaining some sort of hair care strategy or technique.

Maybe you've already uploaded videos to YouTube® and you're sitting there thinking, *"There weren't 50,000 people lining up to see my video…. Where am I supposed to find those people?"*

Look, I certainly didn't have 50,000 people watching my videos when I got started and some of my videos still don't get to that many people, but that's not the point.

The important part isn't where you're at *right now*. The important thing is the direction you're heading and the destination you plan on reaching. To live the life of a Million Dollar Stylist®, you want to have the tools you need to make you getting to your goals a reality instead of just a pipedream. A **website** (one that's made the right way) is one of those tools.

HOW TO SHIP YOUR EXPERIENCE AND SKILLS ALL AROUND THE WORLD!

If you're a skilled stylist right now, I want to tell you something that very few people have probably ever said to you. The fact is, **you're extremely underpaid** for what you know and for what you can do. How does it feel to hear that? What's your reaction to hearing that you are way more valuable than you or the rest of the world currently know?

So, why are you under paid? What exactly is the problem that's keeping you from breaking out and truly getting paid what you are worth for your skills with hair? The problem **isn't** that you don't have what it takes to succeed, and the problem **isn't** that you aren't living in the right town or that you aren't from the right family or that you don't have the right education.

Those are all just a bunch of excuses that people use to keep themselves inside their comfort zone. Million Dollar Stylists® don't make excuses. They don't make them because excuses don't add any value to the world. In fact, excuses only KEEP value from being added to the world. They keep people down, they keep them playing small, and they keep them from actually making an impact.

The real obstacle that stands between what you get paid now and what you are truly capable of making is simply that you haven't made your knowledge and expertise available in ways that an unlimited number of people can benefit from them. Once you do that, **the sky is the limit**.

We've already talked about turning what you know into marketable products like videos and articles, but that's really just the beginning.

There's a lot you're able to help people with that you probably don't even realize. In fact, there's a good chance that as a working stylist, you've probably forgotten more about working with hair than most people will ever even know!

The goal is simply to put all of that knowledge in a package that's easy for others to consume.

The good news is that there are really no limits to how you can do this. Once you get the hang of how it works, you can take all of that skill and know-how that's trapped in your head and release it to the entire world.

A VALUE-CREATING WORKOUT FOR YOUR CREATIVE MUSCLE!

Let's start working your creative brain for a minute. You might find this extremely simple, or it might feel a little bit weird at first. Just remember, your creative brain is a muscle. Like any muscle, it has to be worked out to grow and stay healthy, so that's what we're going to do. I just want to give you an idea of what's possible and show you a little bit about how this process works.

Let's take a straightforward subject like how to do weaves. To you or me, doing a weave might be a pretty straightforward thing. Now, think back to the time **before** you knew the first thing about doing them.

From the outside looking in, it looks like a pretty complicated process. There are a lot of details to get right and a lot of mistakes you could make that could ruin the entire process.

Think about how valuable it might be to someone who isn't experienced to have a video to follow that walks him or her through the process of doing it.

By making a video like this (along with a short workbook, perhaps, that lists out some supplies and additional things to keep in mind), just think how much frustration and wasted time and money you could save someone. Think about how much you can help.

THIS IS WHAT THE WORLD CALLS V-A-L-U-E

You might be thinking, "But hasn't all of this been done? Can't someone just go over to YouTube® and get this information for free?" Of course they can.

In fact, they can probably get the same information in a number of places, but here's the thing…. It goes back to the trust I was talking about earlier. When you have a group of people who know you, like you, and trust you – people who you've become valuable to far in advance of them ever "buying" anything – the reason they'll buy your weaves video instead of watching a free one isn't just because they want to learn how to do weaves. The bigger reason is that they want YOU to be the one to show them how to do it because they **trust** that you will do it right.

Value can come in many different shapes and sizes. It can be delivered in different media and at many different prices. Take your weaves video, for example. That's just one video, right? In a single video, there's only so much you can cover. That's why there are a lot more opportunities to deliver value, even in and around the sole topic of weaves.

For people who really want one-on-one instruction, a complete weaves workshop would make sense. The point is that you can take the exact same knowledge or expertise and package it up in a bunch of different ways.

MOST STYLISTS GET PAID FOR WORKING. MILLION DOLLAR STYLISTS® GET PAID FOR DELIVERING VALUE.

Just think about how that could be. Instead of helping people one at a time and getting paid at that level, you can help 50 people at a time or 100 or more.

As you can see, the possibilities are endless. You'll never run out of problems to solve for people. And as a Million Dollar Stylist®, that's what you do.

In the business world, this is what they call "leverage." Frankly, I don't care what you call it. To me, it is the path to freedom, and it has been the path to living the life I enjoy – one where I can love what I do, help a lot of people, and <u>still</u> have plenty of money and time to be with the people I love!

Getting paid for the actual work you do vs. getting paid for the value you provide are two very different situations. I'm all for being a highly-paid stylist. I think premium fees for premium service and premium talent is **the** way to go, but there <u>is</u> a limit to what someone will pay to get his or her hair done.

As a Million Dollar Stylist®, you can *definitely* push the upper limit on that and get paid what most stylists would consider **a lot** for doing hair.

But eventually, you're going to hit a ceiling of some type. Plus, if you're styling hair, you actually have to stand behind the chair! I love to do hair, but I don't love the idea that the only way I can make a living is by standing behind a chair. There's clearly a limit to the success you can enjoy if you're going to pursue the career of a normal stylist.

But there's **no** limit to the amount of value you can provide to the world, and Million Dollar Stylists® set things up so they get paid on value delivered, not on work done.

HOW TO BUILD A MILLION DOLLAR STYLIST® WEBSITE SYSTEM

Notice how I underlined the word system in the title above? I did that for a reason. Most people think that to take advantage of the "Internet dream," all you need is a website selling stuff. It might look like that, but that's not quite the whole story.

Part of my responsibility in helping you move forward on the journey towards the land of the Million Dollar Stylist® is not to sugarcoat how the journey is going to be. This is a marathon we're talking about, not a sprint. That's why we're building your future around something like hair that you actually love to talk about.

Reaching success is just too much work to take a direction you don't even enjoy. I wouldn't wish that on my worst enemy!

That's why I'm not going to tell you that if you put up a website and put some products on there that a stampede of people will show up within 24 hours. That's just not how it works. If it were that easy, everyone would be doing it. That's why they're not.

In fact, even taking the first step on the Million Dollar Stylist® journey is going to put you in a very select group of people.

The important thing to remember is that your website is going to be part of a SYSTEM. It's a system that's going to connect you to a lot of people all at once: attracting attention, building relationships, developing trust, and solving problems. The website will be doing a lot of the heavy lifting, but never forget that it's only a part of the system; it's not the whole thing.

Once you truly get this, you'll be way ahead of most people you see trying to get attention online. Most people think that the website is the secret. It's not. It's the *role* the website plays in the entire system that makes everything work.

The real secret is the email list. Your website sits there out on the Internet with only two purposes, really. The first purpose is to get visitors to come to your website and "raise their hand" by exchanging their email address for something they find valuable. This could be a video or an audio file that you've created about how to do something related to hair.

Once you have that email address, the ball is in your court. Because from there, the pressure is on YOU to build a relationship with that person. You do that by becoming a valuable force in their life.

That means you send them things that add value, consistently, over time. Eventually, you get to know what the people on your email list are dealing with. You'll get a clear picture of their hopes, their dreams, and their fears. More importantly, you'll begin to see how you could solve some of the problems they face in their life.

Now, when I say "problem," understand that what I mean isn't probably the typical definition of problem. We're not talking about them hating their job or not knowing what to make for dinner.

We're talking about problems that you can help them solve, problems like not knowing how to properly care for chemically-treated hair or problems like not knowing how to choose the right stylist for their weave. Figuring out how to "go natural" could be a huge problem for someone, and you could help them overcome that problem.

As you can see, the possibilities are endless. You'll never run out of problems to solve for people. And as a Million Dollar Stylist®, that's what you do.

You solve problems: big problems, small problems, and just about every size in between. You have the strategy and the systems to do it for a lot of people at once.

Now, how do you earn the privilege of being able to do that for a lot of people? How do you get them to notice you, to hear you, and to trust that you are the one who should be advising them? Well, that's part art and part science, and now it's time to talk about how it all works....

5

THE MOST VALUABLE BOOK IN THE WORLD

We've come to the part of the Million Dollar Stylist® journey that covers one of the most important tools in your work as a stylist. The funny thing is that this "tool" isn't something that you order from a hair supply company. It's certainly not a tool that was ever talked about in cosmetology school. But this tool, without exaggeration, has the power to move mountains. Most importantly, it can take your message to the world in a way that also greatly enriches your own life.

The tool I'm talking about is a book…a book written by none other than **you**. Is your first reaction to me suggesting that you sit down and write a <u>real</u> book is to think something like, *"Me? I'm*

Becoming a Million Dollar Stylist® is about learning a new way to package your value and present it to the world.

not a writer. I think you have me confused with someone else!" Don't worry. The truth is, people far less comfortable with writing than you have become authors of very successful books.

No matter what you think about your future chances of becoming an author, stick with me through this train of thought because I want to dig deep into what makes this tool such a powerful and transformative force in your future.

Think of your favorite book. It could be a book you read as a child, or it could be a book you just read last week. Think about that author of the book. It doesn't really matter if you can remember the author's name or not. The important thing is that you just spend some time thinking about what it means to you when someone says they've written a book. We'll come back to this idea in a moment, so just sit tight.

THE ART AND SCIENCE OF POSITIONING

As a Million Dollar Stylist®, we are in a business where looks matter. I'm not talking necessarily about <u>your</u> looks; I'm just saying that we're in the business of helping people look good, which makes them feel good.

But how does someone who wants to go to a stylist decide which stylist to choose? Some people ask their friends for a recommendation, of course. Others decide strictly on price. Let's just say, for a moment, that every stylist in the world charged the exact same amount of money. How would you make a decision about which stylist to choose then?

Let's say you lined up 20 stylists in a room, and they each had 30 seconds to explain why you should hire them to help you look great. How would you make a decision then?

My hunch is that in that group of 20, there would be a few stylists who stood out to you. Actually, I'm pretty sure that after listening to all 20, there'd be one or two your gut told you were right. How did that decision happen? How did you rule out 18 of your choices without ever seeing how these stylists actually do hair?

There are probably a lot of reasons. Maybe you saw how the stylists looked or how they spoke or how they carried themselves or how confident (or not!) they were. The fact is, your decision was most likely influenced by quite a few different reasons that all worked together to help you get a feeling about the right choice for you.

All of those factors contribute to something that is called "positioning." You may or may not have ever heard of that. Either way, if you're serious about your journey to become a Million Dollar Stylist®, you want to become a serious student of the art and science of positioning.

What is positioning, exactly? Positioning is the place that your clients have reserved for you in their hearts and their minds. In other words, it's the story the people of the world tell themselves **about you** and what you do.

Read that paragraph above again because it is extremely important – so important that I'm going to make a pretty bold statement right now that might surprise you.

You know how I mentioned earlier that your success in the hair industry doesn't have a lot to do with how well you do hair? You might actually wonder what **does** impact your success in a major way.

The answer is… drum roll, please… **positioning.**

So here's the bold statement: **Your future success as a Million Dollar Stylist® will be directly affected (in a major way) by the positioning you secure in the marketplace.** Now that you know the answer, you're probably wondering what that means.

THE TOYOTA® AND LEXUS® STORY

I can make the whole "positioning" concept pretty clear with an example from the car world. You don't have to be into cars to get this, but just think about the difference between a Toyota® and a Lexus®. If you look at the prices, there's a big difference. But if you **are** a car geek and ever happened to look under the hood, you'd realize pretty quickly that Toyota® and Lexus® cars are basically the same! They're even made on the same factory assembling lines.

So what's the deal? Why the price difference? How can Lexus® get away with charging so much more for basically the same car? The answer is **P-O-S-I-T-I-O-N-I-N-G.** At this point, you might think I've lost it because you realize I'm telling that the only difference that allows Lexus® to charge more for practically the same car is **their story**.

Your ability to get your idea into the mind and heart of someone else is an extremely valuable skill.

If that's what you think I said, then it shows me you're paying attention. And that's exactly the truth. The <u>position</u> that you and your products and services hold in the minds of your buyers means everything.

Inside the mind of the car buyer, the story of Lexus® means something completely different than the story of Toyota®. Toyota® means a great quality car at a great price. Lexus® means something completely different. Lexus® is about prestige. Lexus® is about getting something that says I want **better** than average. I deserve luxury, and I can pay for it.

How can they get away with it? Because selling anything is a mind game, and they are masters.

THE GOOD NEWS AND BAD NEWS ABOUT POSITIONING

At this point, you might think that if "positioning" is so powerful, all you have to do is come up with a great story, and you'll have clear sailing. Trust me, plenty of folks have tried that, but that's just not how it works. Yes, the story you tell about who you are, what you do, and why you do it **is** important, but it also has to be true!

Becoming a Million Dollar Stylist® is about learning a new way to package your value and present it to the world. Mastering the art of getting that package to look right (which is what we call positioning) will play a huge role in your future success, but as Million Dollar Stylists® **everything** we do is rooted in authenticity.

This is why the very first part of this book focused on your commitment to be a highly-skilled stylist. You have to be great at what you do. It's not enough to "make it." It's just the price you have to pay to even get a chance to play the game!

So the "bad news" about positioning is that it needs to be built on a foundation of truth. Understand that this holds true for anything I'd ever recommend you do!

You have to be real.

Authenticity is a huge asset in today's world where everyone's been burned and everyone is cynical. To go out there with a sincere desire to be authentic will make you stick out like a sore thumb.

There is good news about "positioning" that you need to understand. The specific place you hold in the hearts and minds of your prospects, customers, and clients is something **you can control.** Yes, it is something that you can engineer on purpose.

Lexus® does it, Toyota® does it, Oprah does it, and Beyoncé does it. And you can do it too.

THE REASON YOU WANT TO
BE GOOD AT THIS

The reason you want to invest the time, effort, and energy required to master the art of positioning **isn't** so you can just sell a lot of stuff.

Sure, success like that tends to come more often to those who <u>have</u> mastered this art, but life is too short to go to all this trouble just for money. That's not what the Million Dollar Stylist® life is about anyway. Money is just one of the byproducts of the larger goal – which is to go out into the world and use what you know and can do to actually make an impact in the world. The goal is to change lives for the better, and do it in a big way!

When you master the art and science of positioning yourself in the marketplace, you ramp up the impact you are able to make. That's why you go through the trouble. That's why you do all of this thinking about who you are, about what you stand for, and about how the value you provide to the world is unique. You do it because when your positioning is solid, it's so much easier for people to receive your message and move forward with you, even without ever talking to you.

In fact, if you do this right, those people will actually search you out for what you have to offer. It is an amazing thing to watch when it happens, so be ready for it!

WEREN'T WE TALKING
ABOUT YOU WRITING A BOOK?

So, what in the world does all of this talk about positioning have to do with you writing a book? That **is** where we started off this chapter – talking about why you're going to write a book.

There are actually a lot of reasons to do it, and we'll cover what some of those are in just a moment. First, understand that becoming a Million Dollar Stylist® is about pursuing a level of living and working that is light years above the average stylist. That means you're going to be elevating your thinking, and you're going to be elevating **doing** in major ways.

Normal people don't write books. Average stylists don't write books. **Million Dollar Stylists® do.** In fact, this book could very easily become the most valuable book in the world to you. It can be that powerful.

Practically speaking, the very process of you sitting down and writing a book about what you do means that you have to get crystal clear on what you do and why.

The time required to do this is worth its weight in gold because the clarity it will give you about what you stand for, who you are here to help, and how you best help them is something that's going to make you far more effective than you'd otherwise be. As I said in the earlier chapter about communication, your ability to get your idea into the mind and heart of someone else is an extremely valuable skill.

If that were the only positive benefit you got out of writing a book, it would already be totally worth the effort. Make no mistake; it **is** effort, but becoming an author has benefits far beyond the clarity it gives you to better communicate your message to the world.

WHAT IT MEANS TO THE WORLD TO BE AN AUTHOR

In today's world, you don't write a book unless you **are** somebody. Celebrities write books. Sports figures write books. Famous authors write books. So what happens if **you** write a book? Instantly, the world's perception of you changes. It's almost like magic, really.

Take any type of skill in the world. If you were looking for an expert in that area, would you search out the person who *calls* themselves the expert or would you search out the person who actually wrote the book about it? Time and time again, it's proven that authors are perceived as experts simply because they've written a book.

Your book not only gets your message into the hands of people who can benefit from it; your book also cements the idea that you **are** somebody in the hearts and minds of people. Of course, you **are** somebody, but when you write a book you actually begin to act like it! And people notice. Trust me, they'll notice.

Just imagine meeting someone at your salon one day when they ask you about your history or how you got into the hair business. It happens every day, right? Most stylists would just take that opening and start blabbing about themselves. But not a Million Dollar Stylist®! You'll just be able to turn around, pick up a copy of your book, and hand it to the person. Now **that** will make an impression.

Just in case you're freaking out that writing a real book is some superhuman feat, let me put your mind at ease.

WRITING A BOOK IS NOT HARD!

It is work, but it's not hard. We're not digging ditches here; we're simply getting our ideas out in a form where they can actually help people.

Writing a book is **exactly** like eating an elephant. How do you do it? You do it one bite at a time! In the case of the book, it's just one step at a time. By the time you break it down into all of the little steps, the whole thing doesn't sound like such a big deal.

It all starts with the people you are writing your book for. What are the issues they're dealing with that you can help solve?

Once you know **who** the book's intended audience is (you could easily use your book to attract clients), then you can ask yourself what's the one BIG idea you'd like to communicate in your book.

In other words, if someone read your book and remembered **nothing** else about it, what's the one most important thing you'd want them to remember? That's your big idea.

From there, you fill in the rest of the book with supporting information, entertaining stories, and more. It's like a puzzle that you put together. You don't have to have it all figured out before you start. All you need is a commitment to actually START!

Getting your book out into the world will make a huge contribution to what's coming next on our Million Dollar Stylist® journey, so it's not something you want to "skip" over. For now, let's move on so you can see what comes next!

6

IT IS YOUR TIME TO LEAD

Today is your day to stop looking for a leader and go out into the world and become one for others. The fact is, you already are a leader on the **inside**. You have what it takes. All you have to do at this point is bring that out into the world where other people can benefit.

How do I know you have what it takes to be a leader? Because we **all** have what it takes to lead. Leading is not about being born with a special talent. Leading is about making a decision that you are going to be the one to blaze the path for others. Leadership is a decision.

Think about it. You've already shown more promise than the average individual. After all, you're reading this book right now. You have to understand that people who aren't going to step out in front and become a leader don't read books like this. Instead, they sit in front of a TV every night, being whisked away to some sitcom or just watching a movie.

You are different. You are here right now reading this. Do you get that? Out of **all** of the thousands of other things you could be doing right at this moment, you have made the choice to invest your time in you. You've chosen to invest your resources in your future success. Understand what that means.

It means that your future ability to lead others will be directly affected by the decisions you make today. Life and success are about decisions.

When I first started doing hair way back in the day, the absolute last thing I ever thought I would be was a leader. No one ever sat me down and said, *"Marquetta, you are here to do great things. You have been given gifts and talents that can transform the lives of thousands of people. Share those gifts and talents and use them well. There are people out there who are depending on you to help them. Never forget what a responsibility and privilege that is."*

Just imagine if someone had told you something like that as a child? How would that have affected your mindset? How would that knowledge have completely altered the way you viewed yourself? It would have changed things in a major way. I can tell you that.

Most of us didn't have the luxury of hearing something like that, so the second best time to hear it is now, today, and then to move boldly in the direction of your dreams. Just in case you've never had anyone tell you, I'm going to take a moment and make sure the message gets through.

YOU ARE HERE TO LEAD OTHERS: TODAY IS THE BEST DAY TO START!

You have to look pretty hard in today's world to find true leaders. There are plenty of examples of people who are *supposed* to be leaders. There are plenty of "leaders" in whom millions of people have put their trust. Sadly, all you have to do is read the news for a few minutes to realize that most of those leaders just aren't real leaders. They're in it for themselves and their actions prove it.

Leadership is not about control. It is not about getting a bunch of people to do what you want. It is not about becoming rich or famous or getting your picture on the cover of a magazine. Sometimes those things do happen to leaders, but that's not really the point of why you lead.

We lead because it's our job. We lead because we have something to offer those who follow. We lead because we are on a mission to make the world a better place tomorrow than it is today. And we're willing to stand up and take the reins to help make that happen.

WHAT DOES LEADERSHIP HAVE TO DO WITH BECOMING A MILLION DOLLAR STYLIST®?

That's a good question. Look around at the current state of our world. The "economy" is struggling; people are losing jobs left and right. The way people used to "make it" by getting a good job and working it for years is crumbling. From the looks of it, there's no longer an easy way to make a secure and stable living.

And yet, there is more opportunity today for people than has ever existed in history… ever!

So, what's the problem? The problem is that this new kind of opportunity is hidden. It's invisible to most people. The opportunity is covered in something that makes it completely unrecognizable to the average individual.

Normal people have not been trained to see this. So basically, while there are hundred dollar bills laying all over the ground waiting to be picked up, the average person is scared to death because they can't figure out how to make a living!

As a Million Dollar Stylist®, you are trained to see this opportunity. You are trained to tune in to all of the "hundred dollar bills" (opportunity) scattered all over the place.

Not only that, you have the tools you need to pursue those opportunities and use them to completely transform your life. All because you can **see what others can't see** <u>and</u> because you have an understanding about what to do next!

That's exciting enough all on its own, but it gets even better because once you are able to see this new path, this new way to "make it," just imagine what happens if you start sharing that with people you care about… and what happens if you share it with people <u>they</u> care about… and so on and so on.

As a Million Dollar Stylist®, you do not allow your lack of knowledge about how to do something become an obstacle to you actually getting it done.

Eventually, you can create huge change by showing tons of people how to see what they are currently missing. This is what a leader does. This is what a Million Dollar Stylist® is all about.

The journey to becoming a Million Dollar Stylist® is about you taking the leader currently on the inside of you and bringing it out to make a major impact on the world.

If you can feel that excitement brewing in your gut right now about the number of people you could help, then I want to let you know that you are in the right place! So let's keep going....

HOW EXACTLY DOES A MILLION DOLLAR STYLIST® LEAD?

The first thing you need to realize is that leadership is something that you **decide** to do. You don't need an Ivy League education, you don't need permission, and you don't need anything special to get started.

It all begins with you making the decision, right here and now, that you have been put on this earth to help lead others and that you're actually going to go about making that happen.

It might sound funny to say, but you can be a leader, starting right now, even if you have no one who's interested in following you yet!

Complaining might feel like you're doing something, but it's really just a waste of energy — energy that you could put towards a much more worthwhile goal.

The general public might laugh at something like that, but that's only because they're used to seeing the "celebrity type" leaders that are all over the news and on TV. Those are not real leaders.

Becoming a leader is about making a decision and then taking action that follows from that decision. In that way, the simplest and most direct way to become a leader is to start acting and speaking like one!

Take a quick look at the world, and you'll see that talking and acting like this puts you in an extremely select group. In fact, it's extremely radical behavior, mainly because we've all been trained (in school, etc.) to look for **other** people to be the leaders. We think that's not something we do, right? **WRONG.** As a Million Dollar Stylist®, you're not going to wait for anyone. There's simply too much good to do in the world and very little time.

So let's get down to the nitty-gritty about how this works. What exactly does this "leadership" hiding inside you look like out in the real world?

TRANSFORMING WHAT YOU KNOW AND DO INTO HIGH-TOUCH, HIGH-VALUE OPPORTUNITIES FOR TRANSFORMATION

One of the most effective ways to help someone create major change in his or her life (for the better) is through the use of coaching, seminars, and speaking. Apparently, the fear of public speaking is pretty high among the list of biggest fears people have. And it's understandable.

With public speaking comes risk... risk that someone might not actually like what you say! This fear of "rejection" has been so worked into what we think and feel about ourselves that it keeps people from ever getting out of their comfort zone enough to actually help people.

If you're someone who's not exactly excited by the idea of getting up in front of people and talking even about something you love (like doing hair), you're not alone.

In fact, feeling anxious about public speaking is actually quite normal. Being a Million Dollar Stylist® doesn't mean you're not nervous, but it means that you'll take action anyway!

We'll talk about the different ways you can turn your expertise into high-touch, high-value opportunities for transformation in just a moment. First, I want to make it clear **why** you would decide to go speak publicly or even put seminars together.

It comes down to **impact**. For the last 11+ years of my life, I've been "talking" with tens of thousands of stylists and other hair lovers using email. Sometimes I send out articles, videos, or just simple updates about what I'm up to in the hair industry.

The relationships I've built with some of my customers and subscribers over the years are extremely special to me – far too valuable to describe in words, but as amazing and efficient as email is, there is a limit to how much you can bond with someone through the computer.

EVERYTHING CHANGES WHEN YOU'RE ONE-ON-ONE OR IN A SMALL GROUP

The moment you're in a one-on-one situation, even when you're leading a small seminar, **everything changes.** The amount of impact you have changes. Your ability to create deep relationships quickly changes. The pace of the transformation you can help someone achieve changes.

I think back to the first few Lace Wig Mastery Training Seminars I held back when I didn't know what I was doing. I was excited to do them, but I really underestimated just how powerful they would be in the lives of the men and women who attended.

There's something about being in a room with another human being and working with them to achieve a specific goal. It's an extremely powerful situation. Over and over again, I watched stylists come into the seminars as their "normal" selves and then leave the seminars as changed people.

They walked out having a new understanding of their true capabilities for achievement. To play even a small role in that is an enormous privilege.

Even now, as you sit there reading this, there are men and women out there who want to learn from you. Maybe those folks are up-and-coming stylists, or maybe they're mothers who want to learn more about making themselves or their children look great. The point is that there are people who will actually get in their cars and drive to where you are to hear what you have to say.

There are people who will gladly pay you in exchange for your help moving them closer to their goals. There are also people who are at a point in life where their futures can be transformed by hearing a few minutes of your message.

BUT HOW DO YOU DO
SOMETHING LIKE THIS?

If the idea of arranging a speaking engagement or even an entire weekend seminar about hair is something that sounds a little bit overwhelming, don't worry. That just shows you are human!

To be frank, there can are a lot of little details you need to deal with to pull off an event like this.

This leads me to a very important principle that will serve you very well on your Million Dollar Stylist® journey. Actually, it's a new habit that you are going to develop over time. It might be difficult at first, but eventually it'll become second nature to you.

The habit I'm talking about actually involves NOT doing something. As a Million Dollar Stylist®, you do not allow your lack of knowledge about *how* to do something become an obstacle to you actually getting it done.

To the average person, that's crazy talk. After all, how could you *possibly* do something that you don't know how to do? On the surface, that sounds impossible, except that people all over the world are proving it's not impossible each and every day.

If you want to join those folks who are doing great things, you simply have to make the decision. Decide that you will no longer allow "not knowing" how to do something keep you from doing it anyway.

The important part is intention and commitment. You start with those two mindsets. One day I woke up and said, *"I'm going to host a seminar for stylists and show them how to make Lace Wigs."*

Did I know how to put on a seminar? No. Did I know how to negotiate a room with a hotel? No. Did I know the first thing about all of the details I needed to take care of up until (and even after) the event? No.

When it came to putting on that first seminar, there were many more things that I *didn't* know, but that didn't affect my decision. I still decided to do the seminar. And now, years later, I thank God that I made that decision.

Not knowing how to do something will only stop you if you allow it to stop you, but you're better than that. You won't be stopped by small details because you will stay focused on the larger goal: helping people transform their lives while at the same time transforming yours.

FINDING THE DIAMONDS AND HELPING THEM SHINE EVEN BRIGHTER!

Million Dollar Stylists® are focused on delivering more value to the world than anyone else. We get paid on the value we provide to the world, remember?

Most people don't realize that, especially the folks who are always complaining about not getting paid what they're worth. The truth is, we're all getting paid **exactly** what we are worth to the world at the moment.

If that's not to your liking, then you are the one who has to do something to change it. Complaining might feel like you're doing something, but it's really just a waste of energy – energy that you could put towards a much more worthwhile goal.

When you're working behind the chair as a stylist, you don't always get to choose everyone who comes into the salon and sits in your chair. So as we <u>all</u> know, you can meet a wide range of people. Oh, the stories I could tell about some of the characters that have come through my door to my chairs!

Some of those people who show up are pleasant to be around and brighten your life while they're in your presence, but some folks do the exact opposite.

Just imagine if you could order a whole room of the type of people who actually make your life better? What if you could show up and be surrounded by 10, 150, or even 400 people who were positive, energized, and ready to live their best life?

That's a pretty exciting way to spend your day, and that's **exactly** what you can do when you figure out how to be valuable to the world using public speaking, seminars, and even personal or group coaching.

You get to work with the best and help them be even better. And you can even get paid well for doing it!

HOW TO JUMPSTART YOUR OWN CREATIVE BRAINSTORM

Everything you do from this point forward begins in your mind. That might sound all fluffy to say but it's not. If you can honestly sit down and imagine yourself speaking in front of people about something you love as much as hair, then **you can make it happen.**

So just take a few moments and really take stock of all of the knowledge that you have to share about what you know. It can take a few minutes to start to get the brainstorm going. In fact, at the beginning, you might not even be able to come up with many ideas.

Don't stop, though; just give it some more time and more thought. It's easy to discount what you know because so much of it might be obvious to you. You might say to yourself, *"Doesn't everyone know how to do this?"* or *"I can't share this type of thing. It's just too basic."*

That's what we all think at the beginning…until you realize that there are many, MANY people out there who know far less than you do. To them, **you are** the expert already, and you can be extremely valuable to them by sharing what you know and what you do.

So please, don't discount your own value. It's a nasty habit we humans have, and it's time that we just all give it up.

You can lead the way!

7

LIVING THE MILLION DOLLAR STYLIST® LIFESTYLE

While we are quickly coming to the end of this book, the journey we're on together really is just beginning. My promise to you is this: if you understand what the Million Dollar Stylist® is truly about and you spend the next 12 months working the strategy that is behind it, **you will not believe** the transformation your life will experience.

I don't know if that transformation will ultimately take you 12 months, 24 months, or even more. The amount of time it takes you really isn't the point. Being on the path is the point.

There are three foundational pillars that will support your entire journey to becoming a Million Dollar Stylist®:

PURPOSE. PLATFORM. PRODUCT.

That's it right there. Those three words are the entire "secret" behind the Million Dollar Stylist® System. I put the word "secret" in quotes because I'm kind of joking about it being a secret.

I really hate that word! Every time someone's trying to sell you a "secret," it always seems to look a whole lot like common sense when you discover what it is, and that's exactly what we've got here in the purpose, platform, and product foundation of the Million Dollar Stylist® journey.

These three P's **are** common sense. The difference is in how you get these things to work together as a system and also what type of action you take to power that system.

So let's start with item #1, your purpose.

WHAT IS YOUR PURPOSE?

I have no desire to be the world's greatest stylist or to spend countless hours doing hair for clients – not even for high-end clients. It's not that I *couldn't* do it; it's just not what lights that fire inside my soul.

What lights that fire, for me, is to teach and train and to find that fire in other stylists all across the world and help them light their fire into a raging inferno.

That's what gets me out of bed in the morning, and it's something I've known, deep down, ever since I started doing hair around the age of six. It didn't even matter that the only hair I was doing was attached to Cabbage Patch dolls. I still knew I loved hair!

Think about what you spend your time doing in your life, especially the things that relate to the hair industry. What are the things that, when you're done doing them, actually leave you with **more** energy than when you began? I'll bet you don't have to think too hard to come up with a short list of what those things are.

Now, I'm not saying that that's your purpose. I would never have the audacity to give you an answer that really only you can give yourself, but what I *will* say is that those things in your life that energize you **are** clues as to what your purpose could actually be.

If I had to define "purpose," here's what I'd say:

PURPOSE LIVES AT THE INTERSECTION OF YOUR PASSIONS, YOUR TALENTS, AND THE NEEDS OF THE WORLD

If you're not exactly sure yet what your purpose is as a Million Dollar Stylist®, don't worry. The clues are all there for you. You just have to take a few steps back so you can see how they might all fit together to give you an answer.

Somewhere near the intersection of what you love to do, what you're good at doing, and what you can do to benefit the world is your purpose. Like I said, don't worry if you're not 100% clear about what that is. Remember, **not knowing** doesn't have to keep you from taking action. In fact, it's been my experience that the only way you're going to get your answers is to actually take action. The answers come in the doing. Remember that.

WHAT'S A PLATFORM?

Think about this picture for a moment. Over on the left side, we have YOU. There you are with your skills, knowledge, and expertise. You're excited to death because you've got all of that energy that's being created because of your clarity of PURPOSE.

The Platform allows you to add value to the lives of many people in advance of them ever becoming a client or customer!

On the right side are all of the people who you can help with what you know and do. When you start out on your Million Dollar Stylist® journey, there's probably nothing connecting **you** with all of those people. That means all the value you *could* provide to the world is currently not able to do anyone but you any good.

The goal is to build a connection between you and those people. I forgot to tell you something about these people. They are pretty cynical. Or, actually, you might call them "street smart."

This isn't their first time at the rodeo and they're pretty sharp. You know that you can help these people. In fact, you are pretty excited about that. There's just one problem.

The problem is that these people don't know that you can help them yet. Even if they did know how you could help them, they just don't trust you enough to actually do something about it. That's strike two right there.

So how do you build a connection with these people that solves all of these issues? The answer is to build a Platform. Let me break this down for you because it's really quite straightforward, even though the effects of this often look like magic.

Just imagine if you had this big list of people who wanted to hear what you have to say about hair. Over time, you send them a lot of very valuable information – maybe articles or videos – or maybe it's just a simple audio recording of you talking. The format doesn't really matter as much as the fact that the information you are sending out is valuable to these people.

Once you've done this for a little while, some magical changes are going to start happening.

First, these people are going to start to feel like they **know** you. On a certain level, that's going to be true. They will have heard from you for long enough that there truly will be a relationship there, even if it's separated by thousands of miles.

The next change that is going to happen is that these people are going to start viewing you as the expert when it comes to hair. This might not happen immediately, but it WILL happen. I know because I've lived it.

Finally, these people are going to trust you. They will accept your expert opinion and take it far more seriously than one from someone else they don't know or trust.

As a Million Dollar Stylist® focused on creating real impact in people's lives, the Platform is going to create the connection with

You attract success to you; you don't chase it down.

those people that will make everything else possible. Like I said, it really <u>does</u> look like magic when this transformation begins to happen. It takes work, mind you, but it's work that is worth doing. And it's work that will pay you back many times over.

Platforms can come in many different shapes and sizes. Maybe your Platform is a simple email newsletter or maybe it's a series of videos you publish on a regular basis. It could even be a print newsletter you send out to subscribers or a podcast or even an Internet TV show. There's really no limit to what you can create.

The important thing isn't really the format, although you **do** want to choose something that you actually enjoy doing. The important thing – the thing that makes the Platform so powerful – is that the material you are sending out is valuable in some way to your subscribers.

The Platform allows you to add value to the lives of many people in advance of them ever becoming a client or customer! Reread that last sentence. If you really **get** that and you go out there into the world and do the work required to make it happen, you will be absolutely amazed at what that will do. It's all because of the Platform – small strategic actions, taken on a consistent basis over time.

That leads us to the final pillar of the Million Dollar Stylist® journey:

YOU GET PAID FOR SOLVING PROBLEMS

Now notice where in this process the "you get paid" step is. It's last. This is how it's supposed to be. Remember, you get paid as a direct **result** of the value you provide to the world.

If you want to make more money, that means you need to find ways to be more valuable! There's simply no way around it. Making a great living doing what you love isn't something you pursue directly. It is simply the natural RESULT of you becoming valuable to a lot of people. Focus on being valuable, and the rest of the details have a way of taking care of themselves.

A lot of stylists don't understand this very core. You attract success to you; you don't chase it down. The reason "chasing success" doesn't work is because we live in a world where everything is energy. You are a bundle of energy, I'm a bundle of energy too. Thoughts are energy; words are energy. Money is energy.

In the world of energy, you are either attractive to certain types of energy or you repel them, so you have to get in the business of attracting what you want instead of the business of chasing what you want.

You can see how this works pretty easily if you just picture a lion at dinnertime out in the wilderness. The lion spots his prey, and he starts to run towards it. Immediately, the prey knows it is being pursued, so what does it do? It runs for its life!

This is exactly what success does when you chase it. This is exactly what money does when you pursue it directly. If you've ever been in a situation where you needed to get your hands on some money, you know it seems like mountains move to keep you from getting it.

Just like it is in the animal kingdom, when you chase something it tends to run away. If there's an exception to this, I haven't found it yet!

This means that if you want to make an amazing living as a Million Dollar Stylist®, you need to learn how to attract success to you so you don't have to chase it.

That's what the Platform does for you. It attracts attention, builds trust, and makes it clear to a lot of people that you know what you're doing.

The trick is to be prepared for what happens next! Because if you're ready, you can transform your entire life in a blink.

Someday, maybe not too long after you get your Platform off the ground, one of your subscribers is going to write in and ask the magic question....

"HEY, I REALLY LIKE WHAT YOU'RE SAYING HERE. I KNOW YOU KNOW WHAT YOU'RE DOING, SO HOW CAN YOU HELP ME?"

And when that question comes, you want to be ready with products and services that can provide the answer. That's why you've gone to all the trouble to create those things like we talked about a few chapters ago.

You've already done the hard work of getting noticed and building trust. Now it just comes down to how you can package what you know and how you can offer people solutions that they can pay you for!

Let's stop here for a second so I can make something clear. The journey to become a Million Dollar Stylist® is about as far as you can get from a "get rich quick" situation. It's not quick, and it's not about getting a private jet!

Being a Million Dollar Stylist® **is** about living life in a way that is RICH. What I mean by that is living a life on your terms, doing what you love, and knowing how to make a great living from it.

That said, I have to warn you. The first time you wake up to an email inbox with money in it, sent to you by someone who knows you, likes you, and trusts you, you will never want to make a living any other way… **especially** standing behind a chair 12 hours a day.

For now, all you have to do is take a single step forward. That's what this journey to becoming a Million Dollar Stylist® is all about. It's about taking one step at a time and never stopping.

WHATEVER YOU DO, NEVER FORGET THIS

Over the course of this book, I've used the word "journey" quite a few times. I did that deliberately. Our current culture is obsessed with getting places. It's obsessed with reaching goals, becoming successful, and "making it" in the shortest amount of time possible.

I'm all for goal-setting, but let's get real: life is a journey, and if you can't enjoy the part of the journey you are on right now, there is no way you'll be any more satisfied when you actually reach your goals.

Trust me. If you're not enjoying it now, you won't enjoy it then. And that is why I strongly encourage you to…

ENJOY THE JOURNEY, EACH AND EVERY STEP OF IT

When the going is hard, enjoy it. Learn from it. The challenges are there for a reason. When the going is smooth, enjoy it, as well, with gratitude for what you've been given. Never look at a problem as a problem; look at it as an opportunity to grow and learn.

No matter what is going on, learn from it, accept it, and keep your eye focused on the future while enjoying the present. And when in doubt, take another step forward.

Living the life of a Million Dollar Stylist® is truly a gift that you can give yourself. Your journey begins now, and all it takes is a decision to begin.

Now is your time to walk with confidence in the direction of your dreams!

ABOUT THE AUTHOR

Marquetta Breslin is the co-founder of Breslin Products, LLC. She is a Licensed Cosmetologist, educator, and author of *The Black Hair Answer Book* and *Chained To The Chair No More*. She has educated some of the industry's top professionals, including Oscar-nominated makeup artists and *Vogue Magazine* Editorial Stylists. Marquetta has been featured in *Sophisticate's Black Hair Magazine*, *BNB*, Business 2.0, CNNMoney.com, NBC, and ABC. Her custom lace wigs have graced cancer patients and Hollywood feature films. She is the creator of systems such as "Lace Wig Training System," "Cutting Mastery," and "Million Dollar Stylist®," which have reached more than 45,000 customers in over 55 countries. She is also a professional speaker and trainer, mainly at live events, such as her Lace Wig Mastery Training Seminar and Million Dollar Stylist® LIVE! For booking information, please visit MarquettaBreslin.com.

Your Million Dollar Stylist®
Journey Begins NOW!

Visit MillionDollarStylist.com for the next step in your journey.

Now that you've discovered the world of the Million Dollar Stylist®, the next step is up to you. Do you continue your life on its current path, or do you take a turn and get on the road to becoming the next Million Dollar Stylist®? The choice is yours.

MillionDollarStylist.com